La seule façon de vivre
est de

Foreword

A good way to picture the basis of a marriage is as a team. Teams usually work well when there are several different factors in place such as corporation, communication, understanding and other similar characteristics. Get all the info you need here.

The Perfect Partner

The Perfect

Tips On Finding The Perfect Mate

Synopsis

Being able to have all these good qualities within the marriage relationship will allow both parties to live comfortably and peacefully with each other and this should ideally be the ultimate goal to look towards achieving.

The Basics

Anyway due to the many difficulties in life this may frequently be very hard to zero in on partaking in the marriage without a few cognizant practices that will assist with keeping the two players zeroed in on the great components inside the relationship rather than on its pessimism.

Most specialists would confirm the way that maybe the main component that ought to be predominant inside the marriage should be correspondence. Great correspondence has been evaluated 100% of the time as the main fixing to develop in the event that the marriage is to have a sensible battling chance in succeeding.

This straightforward yet exceptionally integral asset permits the two players to be completely mindful of every others thought, dreams, discernments, requirements, needs, and a large group of other useful pieces of data that will permit the two of them to exist together, make and keep a solid

relationship that will keep going for the since quite a while ago run.
The capacity to be insistent is likewise one more great quality to rehearse. This component inside the "group" will assist the two players with being more on top of one another's sentiments accordingly making a more giving rather than just taking demeanor.
Everybody might want to be treated with deference and nobility, and this is significantly more significant as the marriage ages. Most couples will more often than not wrongly underestimate one another and this is generally the fundamental driver for dissatisfaction inside the organization. Everybody might want to be treated with deference and pride, and this is considerably more significant as the marriage ages.

Most couples will more often than not tragically underestimate one another and this is normally the fundamental driver for disappointment inside the organization.

Each individual ought to have their own worth framework set up and this is typically shaped as the singular ages from a youthful grown-up into a more developed and useful member in the public arena. Having great qualities set up will assist the individual through life's excursion and will with being directing point for most choices made.

What Is Generally anticipated

Having the option to investigate the upsides of an individual and as a couple would be something that would merit accomplishing for some reasons of which similarity would be the main one to consider.

Having viable qualities won't just make the development of the relationship more certain and serviceable, it will likewise assist with keeping them focused on the relationship through various challenges.

These qualities will assist with characterizing how the two players inside the relationship think, act, and view each other subsequently making it the main impetus behind the relationship.

A portion of the center components that would characterize a singular's worth framework would need to incorporate desire, capability, distinction, fairness, administration, obligation, regard, devotion, responsibility, strengthening,

intelligence, autonomy, persistency, confidence, adaptability and a large group of other connective mental and actual points of view.

Most qualities are made up as the individual carries on with different encounters throughout everyday life or through family esteems being passed on. These qualities are seen plainly through the manner in which a singular capacities in day to day existence and this is an awesome method for checking an individual's reasonableness as an expected accomplice inside a relationship.

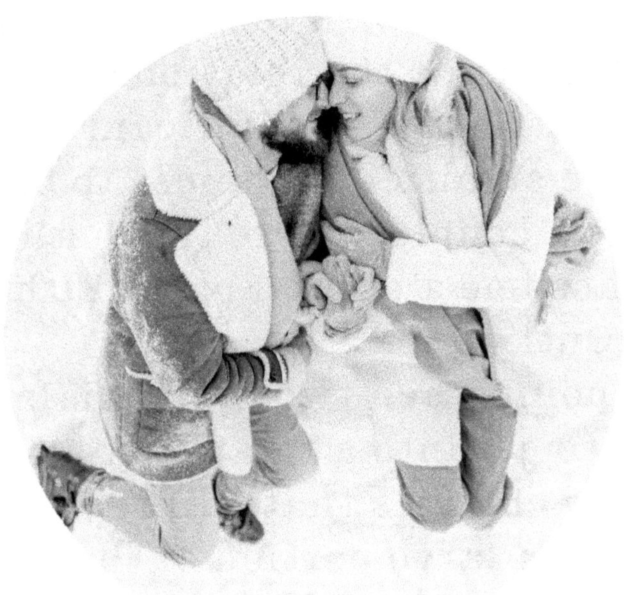

love you

Having great qualities set up and furthermore having the qualities that are viable or commending will assist the two players with feeling more good and loose inside the relationship.
This is particularly significant when there are significant choices to be made as a couple, where the qualities would assume a crucial part all the while. Outline
At the point when two individuals choose to get into a relationship, there are a few changes that will regularly be made and a large portion of these changes are genuinely simple to oblige and live with.

Simply decide

Anyway with regards to rolling out a total improvement, this hope can be somewhat unreasonable as certain things or propensities are difficult to change regardless the conditions are. With regards to components, for example, values, it would be extremely hard to be sure to get the individual to change for the time being or even by any means.

At first it may not be smart to force on the other party every one of the things that are adequate and not satisfactory for the person.

Anyway over the long haul, this is likely smart as it will save a great deal of time and maybe even some sorrow, assuming the two players see that they can't or reluctant to change specific things about themselves.

On the off chance that this is perceived and acknowledged right off the bat inside the new relationship, the two players will actually want to continue on to a more grounded and more engaged level.

Consequently in light of a legitimate concern for keeping rational inside a relationship, the two players ought to be impending with what they will endure and what they are not ready to think twice about. This degree of genuineness will absolutely assist the two players with seeing each other better and to choose if there is any future in seeking after this organization.

It is vital to take note of, that going into a relationship fully intent on attempting to change the other party would be a difficult task and quite often unfavorable to the relationship. Hence the need to choose and acknowledge or leave the relationship before it gets too hard to even consider doing as such. Outline
The vast majority have some thought of what they need they future accomplice to resemble and subliminally search such an individual out throughout the dating game. How Treat See
Not all individuals prevail with regards to tracking down the specific match and now and again will generally agree to the following best accessible choice.

Anyway with a psychological picture immovably set up, the singular will actually want to put forth a deliberate attempt in the correct course and will presumably be in a superior situation to make a decent pick.

Coming up next are a portion of the components that ought to preferably make up the disposition of the best mate:

Development - this is obviously a vital component to forces, as adult people will quite often make more steady mates and are most certainly more solid and experienced in taking care of the different inconveniences inside a relationship.

This will additionally benefit in numerous ways, assuming the relationship ultimately advances into marriage and having children.

Transparency - being open is one more great quality to search for in a mate. The capacity to be unprejudiced and open with regards to all possible things will give the two players to choice to investigate different issues without the danger of getting into a contention or far more detestable influencing the relationship adversely.to investigate different issues without the danger of getting into a contention or far more detestable influencing the relationship adversely.

Truly and honesty - are ideal attributes to have as these too will decidedly affect the relationship. This is particularly helpful when confronted with agonizing choices or circumstances where trustworthiness and uprightness will permit the circumstance to be settled in the most ideal manner while diminishing any effect of antagonism with the said choice made.

Warm - for certain individuals this is an exceptionally regular demeanor to have and communicate, while for other it very well might be something of a test to articulate their thoughts or get friendship without being awkward here and there or another. Summation Meeting individuals isn't something that ought to be trifled with particularly assuming the individual is keeping watch for an expected mate or soul mate. Doing a little research and putting forth a cognizant attempt to all over town will better the odds of having the option to meet with new and intriguing individuals and furthermore contribute decidedly to the errand of observing a reasonable soul mate. Meeting People Probably the most ideal way of guaranteeing the errand of observing a soul mate, who might be considered appropriate, is search out healthy exercises where similar individuals are probably going to be important for. This would surely be helpful to the possible relationship as the two players would as of now share something for all intents and purpose subsequently making ready to different associations that could be possibly similarly charming.

These healthy exercises should in a perfect world be something the individual is completely ready to enjoy, as this would be a vital element that directs the accomplishment of any inevitable relationship found.
It is critical to guarantee all along, the individual is truly sharp and eager to be essential for a specific action and not join basically determined to catch a future accomplice.
Being completely ready to take part totally in the healthy action will likewise permit the person to extend their present skylines regardless of whether there is not a single expected mate to be seen to be caught.
Along these lines making a success, win circumstance and not a possible complete exercise in futility, as this will ultimately turn out to be extremely apparent to any remaining members particularly in the event that the indifference and excitement is exceptionally clear.

A portion of these healthy exercises might incorporate more dynamic games like surfing, plunging, swimming, cruising, kayaking, golf, group activities or less strenuous activities such as bowling, bridge, mahjong and many others.

Synopsis

A lot of conscious thought has to be put into the exercise of picking the right person to share a lifetime with. Mistakes can hardly be something either party can afford to make and neither can either party flit from one relationship to another until the ideal one is found. This will not only be rather time and effort consuming, but will also take its toll on the individual living with this kind of mindset.

Final Thoughts

When most couples make the decision to be part of a committed relationship, there are a lot of mental, physical and legal issues that would have to be dealt with in order for them to take the next step in life as one unit rather than two individual existences.

These issues can sometimes be very complicated and in some cases requiring long term commitments of which it would be very difficult to evade or get out of.

Making a life time commitment to someone is not an easy thing to do and requires a lot of thought and adjustments on both parts.

The changes made are significant and if the relationship eventually runs its course or the notion of calling it quits is very evident, then losses will be incurred on both sides which can sometimes be rather hard to recover from.

Both emotionally and financially, both individual will have to start all over again and this is certainly not a very pleasant experience to have to eventually face. Therefore making the right choice from the very beginning will help both parties avoid such negative possibilities eventually.

Wrapping Up

Most people look forward to being in a relationship that will last for a long time, and in order to be able to enjoy such a scenario, the choice of a partner would be pivotal towards this desired end result.

Hopefully this book has helped.

www.ingramcontent.com/pod-product-compliance
Lightning Source LLC
LaVergne TN
LVHW020547160826
845677LV00015B/4255
* 9 7 9 8 4 0 8 7 2 7 3 0 8 *